Our Hearts are sad.

Dear Oklahoma City, Get Well Soon

America's Children Reach Out to the People of Oklahoma

Edited by Jim Ross and Paul Myers

Introduction by Cathy Keating, First Lady of Oklahoma

Afterword by Robert Coles, M.D.

Walker and Company
New York

Chris, Oklahoma City, Oklahoma

To the children

Many individuals contributed to the creation of this book. We would like to express our heartfelt appreciation to Oklahoma First Lady Cathy Keating for her involvement and her unwavering commitment to the families. Mike Brake, chief writer for Oklahoma Governor Frank Keating, offered valuable guidance, and Bill Welge and the staff of the Oklahoma Historical Society allowed us unrestricted access to their archives, no questions asked. The challenge in tracking down children only partially identified was eased immeasurably by their teachers and counselors coast-to-coast, and we thank them sincerely. A special thank you is also due Anna Myers, for her advice and encouragement, and to Abbie Fiser, for seeing those things only a mother can see. Our editor, Emily Easton, not only gave life to this project but moved more than one mountain to see it completed, and we are substantially in her debt. Finally, we extend our deepest gratitude to the grown-ups who shared their experiences and to the beautiful, caring children, whose loving hugs embrace these pages.

All artwork and letters are now archived at the Oklahoma Historical Society and are used with the society's permission.

To help preserve the character and honesty of their expressions, misspellings by the children were intentionally left in.

First published in the United States of America in 1996 by Walker Publishing Company, Inc.

Published simultaneously in Canada by Thomas Allen & Son Canada, Limited, Markham, Ontario

Library of Congress Cataloging-in-Publication Data
Dear Oklahoma City, get well soon: America's children reach out to the people of Oklahoma/[edited by] Jim Ross and Paul Myers
p. cm.
Summary: A collection of letters from American children to those affected by the Oklahoma City bombing, with statements from some adults involved in the rescue and clean-up operations. ISBN 0-8027-8436-4 (hardcover). —ISBN 0-8027-8437-2 (reinforced) 1. Oklahoma City Federal Building Bombing, Oklahoma City, Okla.,1995. 2. Victims of terrorism—Oklahoma—Oklahoma City. 3. Children—United States—Attitudes. 4. Children—United States—Correspondence. [1. Oklahoma City Federal Building Bombing, Oklahoma City, Okla., 1995. 2. Terrorism. 3. Children's writings.]I. Ross, Jim, 1949- . II. Myers, Paul, 1943- .HV6432.D43 1996   95-44819
976.6'38—dc20   CIP
                                                    AC

Artwork on endpapers by Mathew, who lives in Winter Park, Florida

Book design by Marva J. Martin

Printed in Hong Kong

2 4 6 8 10 9 7 5 3 1

Foreword

This book has its roots in the belief that throughout this tragedy the voices of America's children were all but lost in the torrent of dramatic stories and images saturating the news. Yet their reactions, expressed in both writing and art, cut straight to the heart of the disaster's impact on all of us. They spoke of fear and sadness and of their frustrated desire to help. "I wish I could take somebody's place in the hospital," one child wrote. They vented their outrage and praised the rescue workers. Above all, they wrote soothing words of encouragement to keep the rest of us going. Our goal was to make their voices heard.

We spent many long days and nights sorting, reading, admiring—sometimes tearfully—the countless emotional messages that became the foundation for the manuscript. The statements from adults were selected from nearly 1,000 pages of unpublished personal accounts of the disaster. This collection characterizes a common understanding exclusive of age and illustrates perfectly the need for both grown-ups and children to find shelter and hope in the arms of each other.

We invite you to share that experience.

Jim Ross and Paul Myers
Oklahoma City, Oklahoma

R.I.P
to the young and
the old
whose lives were
sold
Before their time
had come
farewell to
everyone

Roxanne, Montreal, Canada

Katie, El Cajon, California

Introduction

The bomb that struck Oklahoma City on April 19, 1995, killed 169 people—19 of them young children. It was a terrible tragedy, but out of that tragedy came much good. The children of America opened their hearts to Oklahoma.

From the very first days after the explosion, thousands of cards, letters, posters, and banners flooded into Oklahoma. School groups and churches organized letter-writing efforts. Individual children sent their prayers and poems. Each day, hundreds of those messages were placed on the pillows of the rescue workers who were still searching the rubble for victims. Thousands were delivered to fire and police stations. Those messages for the brave rescuers made them stronger. America's children can be proud of the support they gave our rescuers.

Other children wrote to the families of those who lost loved ones in the bombing. They helped ease their pain and dry their tears.

This book includes actual letters, cards, stories, and other contributions from and about children. It proves once again that our young people are kind and loving. They are the hope of tomorrow.

On behalf of Oklahoma, I am proud to thank the children of America. God bless you all.

Cathy Keating
First Lady of Oklahoma

Special Education Class, Anatola Avenue School, Van Nuys, California

In the aftermath of the explosion, the Oklahoma City Fire Department was swamped with mail from kids from all over the United States. Everything received was sorted and distributed to all the fire stations. The stations displayed the items on the walls of the station or rig room to remind them that people everywhere were with them throughout this difficult time. Some of the first letters were sent to the Myriad Convention Center where the FEMA Strike Teams were housed. These were used to decorate the sleeping quarters and the rooms where the rescue workers ate and relaxed.

The Oklahoma City Fire Department deeply appreciates every individual expression of praise or encouragement. Each one was a meaningful reminder of the good that people can achieve together and helped inspire all of us to keep working during this tragedy.

Gary B. Marrs is the Oklahoma City fire chief.

The bombing of the Alfred P. Murrah Federal Building in Oklahoma City demonstrated both the worst and the best of humanity. As a tribute to those who died, we Oklahomans elected to focus on the positive, not the negative.

Possibly the brightest spot of all was the support offered by America's children. Their cards, buttons, candy, and letters poured in. We placed these treasures at the disaster site, in the rest areas, and in meeting places. When we felt down or started losing hope, we had only to look around and the spirit of the nation's children would be with us. What an honor to be admired by America's children!

If it is true that these kids are America's future, our nation is truly in great shape!

Jon Hansen is the assistant fire chief of Oklahoma City.

Amber, Tacoma, Washington

Chantel, Orlando, Florida

Engine 17 to Squad 17: Squad 17—we have a large column of smoke south of (here). You wanta check on that?

Squad 17: That's affirmative.

316 to Dispatch, 316 to Dispatch: This explosion's at the corner of Fifth Street and, uh, Robinson.

620 to Dispatch: Emergency!

Dispatch: Go ahead 620—go ahead 620...(garbled)

This is 600: The Federal Building on Fifth...most of the building collapsed, all the way from the roof down!

603 to Command: Problem here at Fifth and Harvey...people trapped on the third floor.

Engine 4 to Operations: We have people trapped, east side of the Federal Building...

603: I need some more Companies to help with rescue. I need some ambulances here. I got some hurt people!

Oklahoma City Fire Department Dispatch, 9:02 A.M., April 19, 1995

When I heard about the explosion I was in a puddle of tears.

Love,
Cassie
Arlington, Texas

A second bomb scare forced us to leave the building. I was standing outside when I saw two women on the seventh floor screaming for help. I hollered back to try and calm them. They were upset because everybody was backing up from the building. Afraid they might jump, Sergeant Rod Hill suddenly ran back inside to get them. Sergeant Robert Campbell and I followed. When we got to the seventh floor, most of it had been blown away. All that remained was a ledge about twelve inches wide. We edged them along, step by step, until we got to the stairs, then helped them out of the building to safety.

Officer Jim Ramsey is a member of the Oklahoma City Police Department's Bike Patrol.

I hope somebody in the Federal Building that they exploded is alive. That's one wish on a star that I have.

Mickey
Los Angeles, California

I feel so sorry for you. If you are hert I hope you feel better. I just would like to let you know that my dad is driving to Oklahoma City to help the volenters find the people who might still be in all the rubble. I hope that if you lost someone in your family that you will remember only the good times with them. Try your best not to be sad, because you still have them in your heart. They live inside of you. Bye!

From
Mallory
Orlando, Florida

Kyle, Akron, Ohio

Eric, Cedar Hill, Texas

Dad's office was on the fourth floor. He was at his desk when the bomb went off. He was thrown against the wall behind him. He remembers thinking, "That darn computer blew up!" He soon realized he was on a four-foot ledge. The rest of the floor was blown away. Pictures of our family were lying at his side. He picked them up, then called out to anyone who could hear. No one answered. An hour went by before he was rescued.

The fireman asked him to leave the pictures so his injured hands would be free to help him get down the ladder. "Nope. Not gonna do it," he said flatly. After Dad got down from the ledge, a doctor from Shawnee bandaged his hands. Not knowing what else to do, Dad embraced the pictures and started walking north, toward home.

Linda Sanders is a registered nurse at University Hospital.

I know about the bomb. On the news the Federal Building was in ruins. It was so eerie. It looked like a haunted house without walls.

Sophia
Arlington, Texas

When I turned on my TV and I saw all the horror that was happening right before my eyes I thought how horrible this is. I feel so bad for you and all your loses. I hope soon enough all the missing people can be found.

Truly Yours,
Suzanne
Freehold, New Jersey

The rescuers kept on working until ordered out of the building, even at risk to their own health. We treated sprained ankles and twisted knees. We irrigated eyes that were damaged by every imaginable foreign object. We even treated head colds and bronchitis. Incredibly, no matter how uncomfortable or ill the rescuers became, they didn't leave. They were driven by an astonishing sense of purpose that masked exhaustion, hunger, and injury.

Dr. Steve Watson is an Oklahoma City physician.

I wish I could stop time and rewind to make the bad things right. How I wish I could reach out and heal the hurt and make the dead alive. I wish I could find the lost, also.

Giving Hope,
Kirsten
Fayetteville, North Carolina

I wish none of the people died in the bome. My Uncle loved children very very much but he died. If I was in the building I would be rill scared. My Uncle will be up there with your children.

Love,
Courtney
Apopka, Florida

Sarah, Sylvania, Ohio

Emmanuel, San Ysidro, California

I think you are braver than brave itself.

Tara
Croydon, Pennsylvania

"We can't all be heroes because someone has to sit on the curb and clap as they go by."
—Will Rogers

Thanks for giving us something to clap for.

From Trent
South Webster, Ohio

One picture will always stay with me. The sight of a firefighter sitting in a depression scooping out debris with his hands. He was near exhaustion, but he kept going and going.
   That's the way we Oklahomans are: We just keep going.

Randy Britton is a lieutenant with the Lawton, Oklahoma, Fire Department.

On April 22nd, Search Team 3 was assigned to search the YMCA building. While digging through a pile of rubble, we found a crushed aquarium. Next to it, in a small pocket in the debris, I reached in and pulled out a survivor—a small box turtle. Now you have a bunch of grown men giving each other high-fives and celebrating. It may not seem like much, but after three days, finding that turtle was one heck of an uplifting experience.

Philip Miller is a special agent with the Bureau of Alcohol, Tobacco and Firearms in Dallas, Texas.

Dear Courageous Rescuers of the Victims of the Oklahoma Bombing Incident,

I thank you for the help you have done to free the victims of this tragedy. You have been there when you didn't have to, which I respect you for. I really appreciate the work of a man who saved a woman from under the pan-caked floors of the Federal building. He had heard the explosion and hurried his way five miles to get to rescue the victims. What really amazed me is that he drove until he ran out of gas, then ran the extra two miles. He is a true Oklahoma hero and I'm glad to live in the same state with him. A medal should be given to him for his bravery and determination.

My deepest thoughts,
Jay
Blackwell, Oklahoma

(P.S. It would be cool to meet a hero first hand)

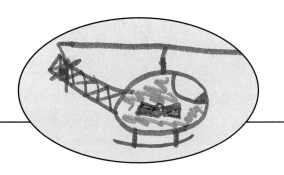

My children have been affected. My five-year-old son, Steven, Jr., was constantly worried about my safety. "Don't fall off the building, Daddy," he said every time I left for work.

One of the boys in my daughter Natausha's class lost his mother in the explosion. My daughter's school sent treats and notes to my station house for the firefighters. Imagine my pride when I saw the note Natausha wrote. In it she said, "Thank you to the rescuers. You risk your lives every day. You are like angels on earth. My dad is an Oklahoma City firefighter, and he is my hero."

Stephen C. Davis is a corporal with Rescue Squad 16 of the Oklahoma City Fire Department.

Boone, Ringwood, Oklahoma

William,
Ashford, Middlesex, England

Dear Mr. Governor of Oklahoma,

My name is Laura, age 9. I live in England. When I heard about the bomb planted under offices and a playground for children I was so DEVASTAUTED. I looked at the paper, and the remains of the Alfred Murrah building made me all cold and pale. I wish I could come over to Oklahoma to help all the parents and friends that lost their familys and friends. If I can help in any way, please let me know.

Love from Laura
Sawbridgeworth, England

People are starting to help others since this tragedy has occurred. I wish I could give the people in Oklahoma everything I have, but that still wouldn't cover up the sorrow. I hope all of the memories of the bombing soon die away and people can go on with their lives. I wish it never happened, but we have learned to be more careful. Remember, there are many people out in the world that care.

Tiese
Freehold, New Jersey

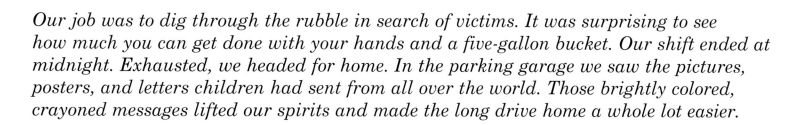

Our job was to dig through the rubble in search of victims. It was surprising to see how much you can get done with your hands and a five-gallon bucket. Our shift ended at midnight. Exhausted, we headed for home. In the parking garage we saw the pictures, posters, and letters children had sent from all over the world. Those brightly colored, crayoned messages lifted our spirits and made the long drive home a whole lot easier.

Dennis Seawright is chief of the Turley, Oklahoma, Fire and Rescue Company.

The heroes I remember best are those who worked in the offices and stores near the blast zone, those ordinary citizens who stopped in the middle of escaping from that terrifying scene to help strangers in peril. They are all my heroes.

Robert Billeg is an Oklahoma City firefighter.

Hello,

How are you? Well, I hope you get better very soon. I can feel your pain and my heart is with you. Sometimes I lay in my bed at night and I think about all the men, women and children who had to go through this tragedy and I break down in tears. I just want you to know that every American's support is with you. I know you can make it through this long dark nightmare. The shock of this incident is felt all over the USA. We are all behind you, and like my grand pappy always said, "If you can make it through the night there's a brighter day!"

Get well soon,
Saleem
Chula Vista, California

here have A balloon

Grant, Worthington, Ohio

To Terry Moore

GOOD JOB!

Collin, Del City, Oklahoma

I have been a member of Ironworkers Local 48 for thirty-five years, and I worked as a volunteer during the recovery process. We shored up the damaged columns and concrete beams to make it safer for the firemen and the rescue teams. Our crew worked twelve-hour shifts constructing trusses out of pipe and angle iron. We threaded this material over rubble and under huge concrete chunks hanging by only one or two pieces of rebar. We drilled anchor plates onto the damaged columns and supported broken cement beams that were ready to fall.

It was a superb team effort. Firemen, other rescue workers, and construction people all joined together to carry the forty-foot pipes into the building, where Local 48 welders welded them securely. Personal safety came second. We were there to help save lives. It was a great coming together in spirit.

Jimmy Crossley is an ironworker employed by Allied Steel Construction Company in Oklahoma City.

Even though I'm only 10 I want to help find those people. The only reason I'm not there is: #1. I'm too young #2. I can't drive. Otherwise I'd be there.

Nikie
Burleson, Texas

Dear Rescuers,
Thank you for helping the victims of the bombing. I know the family members appreciate your help and so does everyone else. It's a sad thing but you guys still go in there and risk your lives to help. All of America and the world thanks you. You are real American heroes to deal with this tradgedy and save the lives of the living and find the dead to bring closure to the families. We all thank you. You're the best.

Thanks,
Melody
Norman, Oklahoma

On Saturday, my husband and I went downtown to help. He said we'd "scrub toilets if they need us to." We spent the day doing an assortment of tasks, from distributing information to giving directions. We spent our final hours helping sort the thousands of generous donations pouring in. I was separating snack items when I came upon a package of pink marshmallow Easter bunnies with a note attached. It was from a five-year-old child, and it simply said, "For the Firemen." To me it symbolized everything: the sweetness of all children, their natural generosity, their trust, their hope.

Schoolteacher Joyce Perkins worked as a Salvation Army Volunteer on April 22nd.

Dear Hero,
I value and appreciate your hard work even more than Power Rangers. I would like to thank you for risking your life. Oh, I would also like to thank the Salvation Army, and blood donors. I hope those hurt kids get well soon!
   Everyone, thanks for helping!

From,
Taylor
El Cajon, California

Taylor, El Cajon, California

Susan, Akron, Ohio

As we were feeding people from the canteen one day, I recall a family of three coming our way. The father was walking with the use of a cane. His wife and three-year-old daughter accompanied him. As they approached, the mother explained that her husband was one of the survivors of the blast and that they were grateful for all we were doing. Their daughter then reached up and handed the canteen commander, Major Brittle, two dollars. The money was from her piggy bank.

Ernest Lozano is the commanding officer of the Orange, Texas, Salvation Army.

All the people who came to help deserve two thumbs up! Every person helping is a hero. The whole country is in pain, yet everyone is coming together to make things easier.

It's strange how it takes a tragedy to make people stand as one.

Amber
Woodbury, Minnesota

Dear Friend,
I heard what happend. I'm going to do a chore for you and
your friends for mony to send, like $1.00 or two. I'm going to
raise mony around the house to do things like clean the
bathtub or a real tough one. I think I could get alot of mony
by cleaning the toilt. Bye for now friend.

Love,
Jenna
Akron, Ohio

Mr. Governor,
I am 8 years old and I live in New York. My heart is
sad about your city. Please see that the 8 bears
go to any child who is hurt or afraid.
                    Your friend,
                    Alexandria
                    Kenmore, New York

*A few days after the blast our command post was evacuated because of another bomb
threat, and we had to stand outside for a couple of hours as a result. During that time,
a woman with several little girls pulled up to the curb to unload items they wished to
donate. Two of them, around two and four years old, walked up to me and gave me
their favorite stuffed animals. They wanted me to give them to little children in the
hospital. Their mom told me that the girls had taken their wagon and gone house to
house, out in the country where they live, to collect items to donate.*

Kim Shirley is the public relations director for the Salvation Army.

Angie, Barberton, Ohio

Monica, Staten Island, New York

One evening, a Red Cross volunteer came by our canteen with a little stuffed bear. She said she was gathering hugs for the children who were so terrified by this disaster. Solemnly, she passed the little bear around the circle of four or five adults who very seriously gave the teddy bear a tender hug. In any other situation it would have seemed ridiculous, but in this instance it was somehow right.

I believe our hugs were felt by those frightened children and that they were comforted by them.

David Boatwright is a volunteer for the Salvation Army.

Dear Governor Keating,

I am 6 years old. I am in the first grade at San Jon, New Mexico. I just wanted you to know how sorry I am about what happened.

I only had $6.00, so I bought a rose bush. It is called a "Oklahoma Rose." I'm sending you a picture of it. My classmates and I are going to plant it on our playground to help remember your little kids and the others.

I think the Policemen, FBI, citizens, and all the volunteers and you are Hero's and very brave. I hope your tears will go away soon and your hearts won't be as heavy.

I really wanted to buy a tree like the President, but I didn't have enough money. I hope you will like the rose bush instead.

I like you. Bye.

Jesse
San Jon, New Mexico

The mourning families, gathered in groups around the site, had tortured faces, disbelief at the horror of it all. Teddy bears, flowers, wreaths, and toys were placed tenderly on the memorial site by the families as a remembrance for what they had lost and could never recover.

They took pictures and murmured where their loved one was sitting at the time of the explosion, what floor, what desk, what they had done that day, that morning. They spoke in whispers to whoever was listening, perhaps just to themselves or to no one at all. Some cried aloud, others wept openly, unashamed. Everybody was crying, some were frozen. Many stood in disbelief by the sheer destruction.

Barbara Woodruff is an American Red Cross volunteer who attended the Family Memorial Service at the bomb site on Saturday, May 6, 1995.

My name is Jeremy and I am 6 years old. I just graduated from Kindergarten. On April 19th my Uncle Scott was killed in the bomb. I don't understand why, but some mean people decided it was time for my Uncle Scott to die.

He was the best uncle a kid could have. He played with me and loved to tickle and tease me. My Aunt Nikki is pregnant. She will have my first cousin in a couple of months. Her name will be Kylie. My Uncle Scott helped name her before he died. She will never get to play with her daddy or see his funny faces or hear his silly voices.

Uncle Scott will never tickle me again, and he'll never say "I love you Bubbs" again. I miss him so much. He loved me and I loved him. Someday, I know I will see him again.

I love you Uncle Scott,
Jeremy
Newcastle, Oklahoma

P.S. I hope you have found a golf course up there.

Robin, Akron, Ohio

Sasha, Oklahoma City, Oklahoma

Dear Firefighters,
You have been very brave to pull all the
people out of the fedral building. That
explosion hit the nation pretty hard. My mom
said your gloves had been tearing up really
fast from the concrete. I felt sorry for
the dogs. I hope they capture the terrorist
soon. I think of you as heros.

Love,
Nicole
Tuttle, Oklahoma

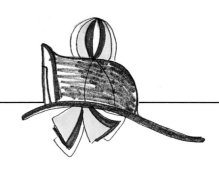

Two K-9 officers and their dogs were invited to attend one of the funerals. When they walked into the church with their dogs, there were a few gasps, then a hush fell over the room. During the service the pastor introduced them and thanked them for all they had done. Several hundred people then rose to their feet and gave these officers and their dogs, Gunney and Arlo, a standing ovation. There wasn't a dry eye in the church. When the two German shepherds detected that their handlers were upset, they raised up and lovingly licked their faces. It was one of the most touching things I've ever seen.

Linda Flowers is a schoolteacher from Tuttle, Oklahoma.

Dear Citizens of Oklahoma,
I feel your grief. Many were lost, but they will never be lost in our hearts. A lot of us would like to scream in rage. We are scared to leave our homes. THAT'S EXACTLY what the bombers want us to do! So do the opposite and other bombers will realize, "it's hopeless, they are too strong of a state!" You are all, each and every one of you, role models to the rest of the world. You will pull through, I know it.

Tiffany
Issaquah, Washington

I understand how sad those people are because my father was killed by a gun on the Long Island Railroad. I asked "Why my dad?" I got no answer. I share the sorrow those people do. When I watched everyone in Oklahoma City as they sang "Amazing Grace," I knew a great many people had been shattered.

Their strength shows that when we fall someone will always be there to catch us. Their strength will comfort our sorrow. I have asked my dad to help watch over the children.

Love, One Reaching Hand,

Karen, age 12
Mineola, New York

My heart aches for everyone who suffered, but especially for the innocent children, who didn't know or care who the ATF was, or what militias are, or what war is.

Firefighter John Clement is a member of Sacramento, California's Urban Search and Rescue Team.

Thomas, Akron, Ohio

Sasha, Oklahoma City, Oklahoma

I viewed the pictures I had taken over and over again as I talked to each rescuer who spent time in the building. All of us relived what we did and where we were on April 19th and during the days that followed.

One rescue worker told of watching a bird build a nest in a shattered traffic light hanging above the intersection of Fifth Street and Harvey. I wondered when our rebuilding would begin.

Penny Turpen James is a forensic photographer with the Will Rogers World Airport Fire Department.

I'm sure the kids in the daycare appreciate what you did. My dad was in a bombing in Somalia. This happened in the year of 1993. His burns are getting better everyday.

Your friend,
Stephannie
Springfield, Virginia

Though this devastating experience destroyed many lives and tore many families apart, I feel that it somehow brought us all together. That day, everyone saw Oklahoma and how we all help each other and care about each other. Before the bombing, we were just another state, but now the whole world has become part of Oklahoma. I've learned so much from this, not only in painful ways, but also in good. Our love for one another has strengthened, and so have we.

Joy
Oklahoma City, Oklahoma

Hello,

I am writing to let you know I believe you can overcome this terror. The people responsible for this will be caught and prosecuted. They are cowards who can't confront their problems. I know it is very hard but there are lots of us out here who care. We support you, and we hope you will soon start back in your normal life. I would be glad to hear from you, to get to know you someday. I am only 15 years old but I have a big heart and there's room for you.

Sincerely with love,
Gabriela
Chula Vista, California

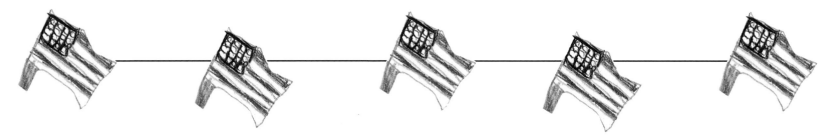

I had been corresponding with a group of kids in Peck, Michigan, ever since a letter they had sent was published locally. They had a school dance to raise money for the injured children and obtained addresses so they could send keepsakes from the Detroit sports teams. They showed support in other ways, as well. At one of the school's track meets, four Peck High School runners dyed their hair the four colors of the Oklahoma flag in recognition of our sorrow. Their generous expression caught on. In nearby Brown City, students tied blue ribbons around every tree, telephone pole, and post in town. It must have been quite a sight.

Jayne Mays is a librarian for Chandler Public Schools in Chandler, Oklahoma.

Joshua, Hartland, Vermont

CHILDREN OF

CARE

OKLAHOMA CITY...

Hope You
get better.

Andrew, Akron, Ohio

It is my hope that when the children of this country look for role models, they will look beyond the usual array of movie stars, millionaires, and sports heroes, and will remember the Red Cross workers, the Feed the Children volunteers, the Salvation Army, and the ordinary citizens who came together on that tragic day. It was they who gave hope and courage to a city and who gave to the nation an unforgettable lesson in brotherly love.

Thomas Phillips is a lieutenant with the Oklahoma City Fire Department. He was on Engine 51 the morning of the disaster.

I wanted to help. I knew I couldn't go to Oklahoma, but I could do something here in Rochester. I took a shovel, some flowers, and an American flag I had in my room. I then went to work building a memorial on my front lawn. I constructed a triangle, put in some potting soil, and planted flowers. I made two peace signs with white marble chips, then put the flag in the middle.

The next morning, I couldn't believe what I saw. Someone had left a basket of cut flowers next to my memorial. Our newspaper did a story about it. After that, people started coming from near and far and within a week flowers stretched from one end of our yard to the other. I promised to leave the memorial up, and light candles every night, until all the missing were accounted for. Each day I watered the flowers.

Even though some time has now passed, I still have the triangle of flowers on my front lawn. A sign I made is there, too. It says, "Keep Up Hope." That is what I still have to say to the families in Oklahoma: Keep up hope. I do.

Joseph, age 11
Rochester, New York

In the future, when I think back to April 19th and the weeks that followed, the shattered facade of the Murrah Building will be eclipsed by the images of piles of letters, hundreds of teddy bears, and the thousands of children's hand prints on posters that covered the walls of the Myriad Convention Center and One Bell Center.

Robert Johnson is a sergeant with the Oklahoma Air National Guard's 137th Security Police Squadron.

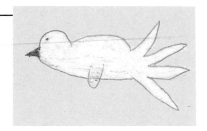

Dear Rescuers,

Thank you. Many victims still live because of your heroism. I watched some of you on TV. You risked your lives to save others. I admire you for your efforts. Will a phoenix rise from the ashes of this tragedy? I think so, an olive branch of brotherhood has been stretched across Oklahoma, the nation, and maybe the entire world! You are in the middle of it, due to your courage. Just one of you has more humanity than the entire heartless terrorist group.

Thank you,
Ryan
Blackwell, Oklahoma

Even if today you feel you will never be able to get back up and start over, you must. Even if you think you have nothing to live for anymore, you do. You have the whole world that cares and wants to comfort you.

So in the name of life
In the name of love
In the name of those who have perished
You shall never forget them, but you will
   move on
Maybe not tomorrow, but someday.

Sincerely,
Caroline
Montreal, Quebec, Canada

Jonathan, Westbury, New York

Afterword

Robert Coles

The preceding pages reflect how extraordinarily responsive children can be to the world around them, how willing to take notice of those in trouble and put themselves in their shoes. In nurseries, a crying baby often prompts other babies to cry. In classrooms, teachers observe their students worrying about someone who has fallen sick, been hurt, is in trouble. In hospital wards, some of us doctors have been surprised, even stunned to hear boys and girls, themselves quite ill, in pain, worrying about one another. These children are able to break out of the self-regard we all have (and to a degree, must have) in order to connect with others. I remember a ten-year-old boy, dying of leukemia in the Children's Hospital in Boston, who kept worrying about a friend who had fallen off his bike and broken his left arm. My patient insisted on sending a "get well" card to that friend. As we who worked on that ward marveled at what we were witnessing, a youthful generosity of spirit and goodness of heart found their expression.

The outpouring of compassion and empathy on the part of America's children prompted by the Oklahoma tragedy of April 1995 ought to remind us how little escapes the attention of our sons and daughters, how quick they are to make distant events a part of their own lives. We live in a time when the psychological troubles and burdens of children are constantly being discussed, and that should well be the case. But we are apt, at times, to forget how strong and sensible children can be, how kindhearted and thoughtful, how morally awake and attuned. As a matter of fact, we spend so much time worrying about the intellectual and emotional aspects of childhood (what children ought to learn, and how they should get along psychologically at home and in the neighborhood) that we may overlook their growing moral capacity, their worries about others down on their luck or hit hard by an unexpected turn of fate. The children whose words and pictures have graced this book were demonstrating their rock-bottom moral capacity, their refusal to turn their backs on others, no matter how far away, who are in obvious need. So doing (so being, it ought to be said), these children become our teachers; they show us how early on we human creatures begin to affirm our essential nature, our capacity for reflective inwardness, our inclination to be merciful, to feel (and give expression to) a heartfelt tenderness toward others in need and under duress. These young Americans have reached out to touch others who had suddenly become vulnerable and endangered, and thereby they reached out to all of us. Surely, upon turning the pages of this book, we will be proud of what the tragedy in Oklahoma brought forth: an outpouring of soulful concern from a nation's sons and daughters that mightily affirms all of us, that does us proud spiritually.